The Prestige

Doncaster 1

Independents - The First 30 Years

Roger Holmes

© **2005 Venture Publications Ltd**
ISBN 1 898432 61 9

Cover: The author's all time favourite bus, Felix Motors No. **26**, a splendid AEC Regent III with all-metal bodywork by Charles Roberts, was photographed in 1957 when nine years old. It was still immaculate and in 1962 was sold to Samuel Ledgard, in whose fleet it gave further service until the West Yorkshire Road Car takeover. *(Author)*

Rear cover: One of a pair of Leyland-bodied PD2s new to Severns in December 1949, **JWR 981** carries the later standard livery with Severn's "S" roundel. It is shown on hire to Leon for use on the special service to the Air Display at Finningley. *(Author)*

Inside front cover: Plaxton bodied Bedford OBs were not as common as the Duple variety. New in 1949, Leon's **KRR 980** still looked smart when photographed at Glasgow Paddocks bus station in 1961. **RD 4340** was an AEC Regal 4 that had been new to Reading Corporation in 1933. After a spell with the War Department it passed through several hands before arriving with Dodd in 1948. Some months later it was sent to Brookes of Dinnington for fitting of the body shown in the picture, acquiring a 7.7 AEC oil engine at the same time. *(Both: Author)*

Inside rear cover: **EWU 380**, the second of Blue Line's Park Royal-bodied wartime Guy Arab 2s, looks slightly down at heel in a 1958 photograph taken in the depot yard a mere four months before the vehicle was sold to a showman. *(Author)*

Title page: The first new double-decker supplied to a Doncaster independent was Felix No. **15** (**CWY 758**). Here it is shown in wartime trim at a time when firms were discouraged from showing place names on destination blinds. The Corporation had always used the route number 23 for their Stainforth route and the independents now followed suit. There was no municipal service to Thorne, but those firms running there now styled it 24. This 1941 picture shows Miss Phyllis Thompson, the first woman in the country to be licensed to drive a double-decker. She subsequently married Edgar Whittaker, who became manager of the firm on Ernest Parish's death in 1957. *(Author s Collection)*

Below: Samuel Morgan's "Gwen" fleet and most of his staff in the yard at Stainforth circa 1926. Mr Morgan is the portly figure in the hat towards the left of the picture. **WT 8287** on the far left is a 1925 Reo, the next vehicle is probably a Chevrolet, then comes **WU 8460**, a Reo new in 1926. Two Vulcans follow, **WU 3691** of 1925, and **WT 1240**, a 2-ton of 1923 that had been new to George Ennifer. *(Author s Collection)*

>> *Opposite page:* Harold Wilson's wartime Park Royal-bodied Guy Arab 2 had acquired new headlamps and an Indian's Head mascot by the time of this 1950 photograph. Otherwise it looks original externally. *(James Firth)*

FOREWORD

Perhaps a long and abiding interest in buses stems from a traumatic experience when, as a very small boy, I was confronted by the brutal, gleaming magnificence of a brand new Dennis Lancet of Yorkshire Traction with its oh-so-impressive radiator shell. Despite this, independents have always been my favourites, and Doncaster was the place to savour them in all their multi-coloured glory. And then my mother's relations all lived in the village of Stainforth, that hotbed of independent activity, and bus journeys there were something to look forward to. Perhaps one of those hollow rattling Gilford PF166s would turn up, or an ancient TD1, a TSM Express perhaps or a Maudslay. Then there were the AEC Qs with that strange sound, as if they were chain driven, or the little AJS Pilot with the Gardner engine. And this was just one route of several, all full of interest and diversity.

These concerns have fascinated many enthusiasts, and it is time they were celebrated in book form. Their story over almost 60 years shows that smaller family-owned firms survive best by cooperation rather than competition - something which eluded the boneheads who framed transport policy in the 1980s. This volume attempts to show where the individuals concerned came from, how they consolidated their positions and how they provided an admirable service for the folk in the areas in which they operated. Their individualism and hard work are much to be admired, and their idiosyncrasies are to be savoured.

The difficulties of obtaining film in wartime and the early postwar period are a matter of great regret, and recourse had to be made to respooled ex-RAF Film, or sometimes paper negatives which cannot be printed nowadays. Consequently some pictures have been included for their great historical interest rather than their technical merit.

Mike Fowler and Tony Peart, who have written articles on several of the independent operators, have kindly checked the manuscript, and I'm indebted to Roy Marshall, who has offered some amendments. Thanks too, to my friends Geoff Clarke and Jim Firth for permission to use some of their photographs. Jim, too, allowed me access to his extensive ticket collection. Thanks also to Dave and Mary Shaw for reading the proofs, and to John Banks, for his enthusiasm, his encouragement and his technical expertise.

Roger Holmes
Stalybridge
May 2005

INTRODUCTION

In the early years of the 20th century Doncaster was on the whole a contented sort of place. It had the massive railway works of the GNR, its racecourse and its municipal tramway, together with a popular, thriving market which attracted customers from the villages in the area, who were mostly brought in by wagonettes. Then the colliery companies decided that the time was ripe to exploit the deeper end of the Barnsley seam. Sinking of pits began in the surrounding district, with Hatfield Main (actually in Stainforth) going into production in 1920, others following during the early twenties. Mining families came from various parts of the country, and pit villages sprang up rapidly to accommodate them. This activity coincided with the increased availability of motor vehicles and people to drive and maintain them following the end of the First World War. Doncaster Corporation's Tramways Act did not empower it to run motor buses. A Private Bill had to go through Parliament, which took some time, finally being passed in 1922.

In the meantime enterprising individuals, largely based in the villages, began running all sorts of conveyances: convertibles, charabancs, strangely constructed buses of seating capacities from 6 to 32. Some began in 1920, or even earlier, and Doncaster, mindful of the trade they were bringing in, bowed to the inevitable and began issuing licences in 1921. In those early days it was a free for all, some licensed, some not or with County or Bentley licences, supposedly using the "Return Ticket" scheme.

Thomas Potts, the long-serving Doncaster manager, always regarded the private operators as "pirates", which was hardly fair, since these were the people who established the routes before the Corporation owned a single motor bus. However, unlicensed operators, the true

Above: Ford Model T charabanc **WY 1454** of January 1922 is believed to have been Robert Store's first bus. It was later given a bus body and served for four years before being sold on.

Below: This 14-seat Guy, **WT 6858**, was new to Ernest Parish in October 1924. He had already adopted the Felix name and the cat motif. *(Both: Author's Collection)*

THORNE HATFIELD & DONCASTER

FELIX

"pirates", did exist right through the 1920s and into the early thirties.

The nearest large operator, Barnsley & District Traction Company, came into Doncaster on two routes, but were concentrating on developing their own local services and did not have an operating base in the town until much later, after acquisitions. Memorably, after the Road Traffic Act, the local independents "saw them off" east of the town.

Nothing more is known of Kemp & Jepson, who were said to have pioneered the Stainforth route with a 14-seat Crossley. An early operator, Doncaster-based, was Messer & Blythe, in 1921 running to Stainforth and Rossington with about half a dozen buses and charabancs including a couple of early AECs. In September of that year the company was sold to Doncaster Motor Services Ltd, whose prospectus carried a grandiose scheme to cover nearly all the routes from the town. In turn this firm's licences were transferred to W T Underwood, with at least two new AEC buses, in 1922. Doncaster, though, would only issue licences to Underwood which were valid until their own buses arrived, so WTU had then to withdraw from these local routes.

All licensed buses had to be submitted for annual inspection, and it is illuminating to read some of the reasons for rejection:

Radiator to be repaired;
Rear seat taken out and new bolt fitted;
Emergency door to be provided/altered;
Front wheel tightened;
Footbrake repaired and resubmitted;
Plate to show correct number of passengers;
Re-submit when new body fitted.

As the badly maintained Model Ts and the ancient charabancs wore out, many owners could not afford to replace them and dropped out. Nevertheless, in a letter to the Traffic Commissioners in January 1931, the Town Clerk listed 145 licensed buses belonging to 21 proprietors (excluding those of the companies licensed in other areas, such as Barnsley, Rotherham and Scunthorpe). He also named 20 operators of unlicensed omnibuses. Some were known "pirates", but mostly these were used on works or colliery contracts, or private hire.

By the middle of the 1920s the position had stabilised. Protective fares over the tramway routes were introduced. Operators had to publish a timetable and stick to it. The pattern of joint operation which existed until the late 1970s had been largely set. Even on joint services some owners listed only their own times, though the local press published complete timetables as best they could, and the locals, the main users, always knew when the bus would come. Timings and shares were jealously guarded, which was to cause problems later when postwar housing had to be served. Fighting between drivers and prosecutions for dangerous driving and "cutting-in" gradually disappeared.

The scene was set for the 1930 Road Traffic Act, which took licensing out of the archaic systems of local authorities and placed it in the hands of Traffic Commissioners. All the owners mentioned in the sections following had some or all of their applications approved as a result.

Services to the east of the town terminated around Christ Church from early times, which was convenient for the market, reasonable for space but rather exposed. Those to the south and west used Waterdale, which became rather cramped, particularly on Saturdays, so they were moved to a bus station in nearby Glasgow Paddocks shortly after the war. This resembled a shanty town, but at least provided shelter. Independent services to the north were less fortunate. Originally housed in a strange concrete structure on stilts, adjacent to the North Bridge, they were then transferred to Marshgate, possibly the most awful bus station in the country. It sat at the end of a cul de sac, overshadowed by the North Bridge on one side and flanked by run down housing on the other. Access to the town was via a long flight of stone steps, then there was a quarter-mile walk over the often windswept bridge to reach the town.

The 1930s was a time of stability, with timings and joint services established, and the proprietors gradually replaced the smaller vehicles of the previous decade with full-sized buses, many bought new. One or two concerns began converting their fleets to diesel power (or oil engines as they were then called). The outbreak of war brought problems, blackout

Above: Severn's only Vulcan was **WY 6908**, a 2T model with Bracebridge body, new in September 1923. A 26-seater, its capacity was reduced to 20 within a few months. It ended its career as a lorry in Bolton.

Below: **WY 509** was one of the two AEC buses new to Doncaster Motor Services in 1922, which soon passed to W T Underwood, of Clowne. *(Both: Author s Collection)*

conditions, reduced services leading to overcrowding, and vehicles requisitioned by the War Department or for use as ambulances. Double-deckers had to be found, and the only ones then available were hardly in the first flush of youth. Service personnel were no respecters of PSV Regulations. Early evening departures from Finningley aerodrome into town had to be seen to be believed - typified by an elderly TD1 with airmen standing both downstairs and upstairs, on the stairs themselves and on the rear platform. As the bus laboured up the hill into Doncaster, one by one the intrepid airmen baled out on to the road (on single-deckers they opened the rear emergency door to perform this manoeuvre).

The immediate postwar period had its own problems. Timetables were restored but, after heavy wartime use, some of the patched-up buses were worn out. One or two proprietors had earlier placed forward orders and were able to take delivery of new vehicles from 1946 onwards. Most, though, went looking for reasonably serviceable examples from municipals or larger firms. Some extraordinary machinery, including conversions, took to the road, as will be shown later. It was an enthusiasts' paradise, though the fitters and the passengers would hardly agree. By 1950 new buses were arriving, including coaches to meet the demand for private hires and excursions.

OPERATORS EAST OF DONCASTER

THE STAINFORTH ROUTE

The busy waterway of the River Don Navigation, linking South Yorkshire with the River Trent, passed through the village of Stainforth, where numbers of individuals were involved in the waterborne traffic. The Parish family, among others, had interests there.

Then in 1920 Hatfield Main colliery went into production. Scores of houses were built, and a complex pattern of bus operation to and through the village began. Seven licensed operators are known to have set up there, five in East Lane, and this included some who operated elsewhere. Pirating was rife: one man, Robert Jackson, described in court as a "persistent pirate", was known to be working from 1923 to 1929.

An early operator was Mrs Alice Roe, who came in from Goldthorpe via Doncaster on a West Riding licence, and who in October 1920 obtained licences from Doncaster (Waterdale) to Stainforth for a 15-seat Vulcan chara and an 8-seat Ford. By 1923 the firm was Roe & Connor and the licence was extended to Fishlake on Saturdays. By 1926 Connor had gone and the firm moved to Fishlake. In 1931 Walter Roe was in charge, he later moved into the Anchor Inn there, and this service was extended to Sykehouse. Stock included a Reo, a GMC and a Thornycroft. In October 1938 Roe's Dunscroft and Sykehouse services were sold to T Severn & Sons, together with two Maudslay ML3s and two Albions, one a nearly new Barrass-bodied Valkyrie (Barrass was a Stainforth coachbuilder).

In April 1921 the Primrose Charabancs began running on Saturdays with two Maudslay charabancs and a 14-seat bus. This was short-lived and the owner, H H Bone, subsequently became a Doncaster councillor.

Samuel Morgan, one of the East Lane residents, who called his buses "Gwen", after his daughter, began his Stainforth service in June 1921 with a 14-seat Ford Model T; another followed, then a Fiat, a Chevrolet and a Reo. His fancy then turned to Vulcans, owning five in all. The route was extended to Dunscroft, and he and Robert Store (q.v.) jointly developed a Doncaster to Goole service. Samuel Morgan Ltd was formed in July 1928. For some time it had been known that Samuel was not in the best of health. In December 1927, Barnsley & District, eager to get a foothold in this area, offered to buy him out. Doncaster refused to transfer the licences. In 1929 Robert Store wished to take over the company. In a letter to the Watch Committee, Doncaster manager Thomas Potts was scathing about Store ("he can't afford to buy"), and alleged that Store was acting as an agent for a big company (Barnsley & District?), which was very doubtful indeed.

Richard Wilson (see Armthorpe section) adopted a different tactic. He bought the Samuel Morgan Ltd company and continued trading under that name, then transferring his own Doncaster - Armthorpe licence to the company and putting his Blue Line fleet name on the buses. Routes involved were Doncaster

Above: This early vehicle of Samuel Morgan's is believed to be the 14-seat Chevrolet **WT 6320** of 1924.

Below: **YG 642** was Store's Dennis Lancet, new in 1932 with a lightweight Barnaby body. Three years later it gained a Gardner 4LW engine and survived with Store, slightly rebuilt, for 21 years. It is shown towards the end of its life in a photograph on page 28. *(Both: Author s Collection)*

- Stainforth and Dunscroft and Doncaster - Goole, and there were probably three Vulcan and two Reo buses at the time. Samuel's son Cliff worked for Blue Line for many years afterwards.

Robert Store

Store's vehicles ran under the fleetname "Reliance" and were pale green with cream window surrounds and blue waistband. The limited company was formed in March 1934.

Although it is not now possible to substantiate it, locals in the village claimed that Robert Store had gone to Australia as a young man, returning with enough capital to set himself up with his first bus, a Ford T chara. Almost every year in the 1920s he purchased a new bus, including two Chevrolets, two Reos, a Thornycroft and a Dennis G. The Doncaster - Stainforth service was extended to Dunscroft and in 1926 the Doncaster - Stainforth - Goole service began, jointly with Samuel Morgan. His first big bus was an AEC Reliance, new in 1931. Its chassis number and this late date almost certainly indicate that it was one of the 20 Model 426 chassis built for the South American market which remained unsold and were converted to Reliance specification. During the war it was rebodied by Barnaby. Rawcliffe Bridge, on the way to Goole, had a strict 5-ton weight limit which was a problem for the operators. Store had a Dennis Lancet built with a lightweight Barnaby body, and purchased a third-hand AJS Pilot forward-control 26-seater in 1934. After withdrawal it was used as a store shed in Papworth's scrapyard for several years. What a preservation project it would have made, especially as Store had had it fitted, like the Reliance and the Dennis, with a Gardner engine. Then came a Bedford/Barnaby, a Leyland Cheetah with a Barrass body and a delightful little Barnaby-bodied Dennis Falcon. In 1939 Store launched a market-day service through rural countryside to Kirkhouse Green.

An interesting sideline is that Barnsley & District in 1929 bought out Richmond's Moorland Bus Service, which was established on a route between Thorne and Goole. On the strength of this they began operating between Doncaster and Goole on an hourly headway in

August 1929. In June 1931 the now Yorkshire Traction's application to the newly established Traffic Commissioners to renew the licence (now two-hourly) was granted, the intention being to link up with East Yorkshire's Goole to Hull service. All the independents lodged an appeal, which was upheld in January 1932. Figures of passengers carried were quoted at the appeal: Store 433,600, Morgan 240,000, Yorkshire Traction 91,300.

The advent of war brought problems. The through service to Goole had to be discontinued. Passengers had to travel on the Dunscroft service and change at the Fox Inn in Stainforth. To facilitate this Hopley & Richardson's Majestic service from Goole was extended from its Thorne terminus. Moreover, what had been a regular 15 minute headway was cut back to every 40 minutes. More capacity was urgently needed. Leeds City Transport was shedding non-standard vehicles and Store obtained AML 996, an AEC Q-type double-decker, which immediately had platform doors fitted. Tales could be told of this remarkable bus and its sister at Blue Line, but it served well for nine years. An ancient, creaky Reliance followed before a wartime Guy Arab arrived in 1944. An ex-Burton on Trent prewar Guy and a Bedford OB/Mulliner bus came along later.

Store's business was sold in April 1949 to the Wilson family, but continued as a separate entity with John Wilson, Richard's brother, as Managing Director, under the holding company Morgan & Store Ltd. This afforded the Wilsons an operating base in Stainforth, which was served by several of their routes. On order at that time was a Meadows-engined Guy Arab 3 with Barnaby double-deck body (very similar in looks to contemporary Roe bodies) and two Barnaby-bodied Leyland Comets, the second of which was the last to wear the distincive Reliance livery.

T Severn & Sons

Fleetname "Cressy" with the colours French grey and white/pale greyish green relieved by light green, later green and cream. The limited company was formed in March 1933.

Thomas Severn came from Cresswell in Derbyshire, marking this by using the

Above: A view of the Store "Reliance" fleet in what remains of a photograph taken in 1949. From left to right are **EWU 374**, a Guy Arab II with Park Royal bodywork; **HWX 3**, a Guy Arab III bodied by Barnaby; **WX 8373**, a Barnaby-bodied AEC Reliance; **YG 642** with bodywork by Barnaby on a Dennis Lancet chassis; **ENT 910**, a Guy Arab III with Barnard bodywork, believed to have been on loan from Blue Line; **BWY 978**, a Leyland LZ2 with Barrass bodywork; **GAT 226**, another Dennis - this time a Falcon - with a Barnaby body; and **EDT 409**, a Mulliner-bodied Bedford OB. *(Author s Collection)*

Below: **WX 8373**, Store's late AEC Reliance, new in July 1931, is seen with the Gardner engine it gained in 1937 and its wartime Barnaby rebody. The photograph dates from 1948. *(Author)*

fleetname "Cressy", current until the war years. He began delivering coal from an address in Bentley, converting his lorry into a bus at weekends, subsequently moving to East Lane in Stainforth and later to larger premises in Silver Street. By April 1922 he was running to Stainforth with a 14-seat Ford, replacing this a year later with a larger Vulcan. In 1924 he extended from Stainforth to Thorne and also obtained a licence for the "Top Road" route from Doncaster to Thorne via Edenthorpe and Hatfield. The fleet grew rapidly, becoming the largest of the local independents in the area. Throughout the 1920s he bought no fewer than nine Leylands, from Z5s to a PLSC1, including two impressive Lionesses. There followed five Lancias, two Saurers which weren't kept long and three Thornycroft A6s. By 1931 he had ten licensed buses, mostly 20-seaters. Thomas had four sons and three daughters, one of whom, Mary, married Ernest Parish of Felix. Bigger buses came in the 1930s, all bought new: Leyland Lions and Tigers, and AECs including three Regal 4s. The takeover of W Roe in 1938 brought two Albions, a PMA28 and a Valkyrie into the fleet, both of which were later impressed into government service, as were two Tigers and a Regal coach. The last prewar delivery was a Barnaby-bodied Albion Victor in 1939, which may have been a W Roe order. For a short time in the late 1930s fleet numbers from 1 to 13 were carried. At some point, CWT 391, the third Regal 4, was fitted with an oil engine, but apart from that all the prewar fleet were petrol-engined, and this continued with the first double-deck purchases in 1939: two elderly Leyland TD1 lowbridges, originally Birkenhead Corporation but via Wilts & Dorset; these were followed later by another one from West Riding. A couple of stop-gaps, the ex-Felix Dodge and Dennis Lancet didn't stay long, nor did a Bedford OWB. Three Massey-bodied Guy Arab 2s arrived, one in each year 1943/4/5. Around this time the livery changed to a straightforward green and cream.

The route to Thorne Moorends, shared with Felix and Harold Wilson, had some journeys which used the direct road between Hatfield and Thorne, with others going via Hatfield Woodhouse. Not far away RAF Lindholme was established in 1940, and some of the latter journeys were diverted to serve the camp.

With few exceptions all Severn's postwar fleet were Leylands, beginning with a pair of PD1s, then three Leyland-bodied PD2s and four PS1s: two Barnaby buses and two Yeates-bodied coaches. After just five years service the first Massey bodied-Arab 2 went to Barnaby's for a new body, as did one of the LT7s, which was fitted with a PS1-type engine.

William Lowe managed to sell his "Mabel" bus service twice. In 1923 he began operating to Stainforth, extending to Thorne the following year, also running between Stainforth and Thorne Moorends on Mondays, Wednesdays and Fridays. In November 1926 his Doncaster to Thorne service went to Severns, but he retained one bus and the Moorends route went to Blue Line in May 1932. Severn took no buses, but a Bedford WLG went to Blue Line.

THE ARMTHORPE ROUTE

Arthur Braim

Braim's fleetname was "St Leger Coaches" and his colours were green and cream.

Arthur Braim was a pioneer operator to Armthorpe, well before the colliery was opened. His 28-seat charabanc appeared in May 1920, when the roads were largely unmade. Subsequently he is known to have operated two 14-seat Fords, two Chevrolets, a Fiat, two early Leylands and a Studebaker. At the outset of war his "St Leger Coaches" business was offered for sale and was purchased jointly by the three other operators on that road, Doncaster Corporation, Blue Line and Felix. The sum of £5,500 was paid for the business.

The existing fleet was valued at:

FW 5174, Bedford WLB new 18.8.34, £30; kept by Braim for use as a lorry
WX 7898, Leyland LT2 new 2.7.31, £75; sold.
DT 7755, Leyland LT7 new 1.9.36, £240; sold.

R F H Wilson

The fleet name was "Blue Line" and the colours blue and cream/two shades of blue. The limited company (Samuel Morgan Ltd) was formed in March 1929.

Above: **CWY 881** was a Barnaby bodied Albion Victor PK 115 new in February 1939. It was the second No. 1 in Severn's short-lived 1930s fleet-numbering scheme. Severn had never previously been an Albion customer, and this vehicle may have been ordered by W Roe of Fishlake, whose business passed to Severn in October 1938. *(Author s Collection)*

Below: **FWW 19** was one of a pair of Barnaby-bodied Leyland PS1s delivered to Severn in November 1947. Both were sold to Armstrongs of Ebchester in 1956. This photograph was taken on 20th September 1952. *(Author)*

Richard Wilson came on the scene in 1922. Work was progressing on Markham Main colliery, and new houses were being built. With his little Ford Model T, he began a service to Doncaster, initially via Edenthorpe as the direct road was in no fit state for buses. He was also involved with taking miners to another pit until Armthorpe went into full production in 1925. A bold decision led to him taking a lease on Wood Lea Farm and buildings, in the old village, to use as his base, leading to its purchase in 1929. A varied assortment of buses included another Ford, an SPA, a Federal Knight (named Blue Bird), and a Reo (named Blue Canoe). The first double-decker for a local owner appeared in June 1927. This was UK 2399, a 6 wheeled Guy BX, an ex-demonstrator, which was believed to have been at the 1926 Motor Show. It trundled faithfully back and forth on the route until some time in 1933 when it suffered serious engine failure. Its replacement was just as remarkable, a 1928 Guy FCX which had started life with the Public Omnibus Company, passing to the LGOC as fleet number GS14.

The body was destroyed in the LGOC's West Green garage fire, but the chassis was salvaged, given a new Hall Lewis body and sold to the West Hertfordshire Motor Service. In November 1933 it appeared in Armthorpe and some time later it received a Lycoming engine, probably obtained from a Gilford. It had an extensive body rebuild during the war and soldiered on until 1949. There were a couple of Reo Pullmans, one of which survived until 1945, together with Vulcans and Reos from the Samuel Morgan fleet and W Lowe's Bedford. For the Goole route, with its 5-ton limit on Rawcliffe Bridge, a pair of lightweight Gilford PF166s with Park Royal 32-seat bodies (Gilford's last fling) were bought. A third came secondhand, so that Blue Line owned three of only four PF166s ever built. This was the closest to standardisation reached until postwar times, as a Maudslay ML3K, a Foden SG4, a Bristol B, a Gilford 168OT and a TSM Express (both the last two being rebodied by Barnaby during the war) made up the rest of the fleet. With more capacity needed in wartime Wilson bought the sister AEC Q to Store's from Leeds City Transport. This was UG 6511, recently modelled by EFE in its Leeds livery. More odds and ends included a Leyland Lion PLSC1, another Bristol B (which was fitted with perimeter seating), an AJS Commodore, a Dodge SBF, and two rebodied Daimler CF6s from a local coach operator. The arrival of wartime Guy Arabs, two with Park Royal bodies and a Northern Counties example, changed all that. From then on Guys became the purchase of choice.

Two Guy-bodied Arab 3s with Meadows engines (subsequently rebuilt with Gardner 5LWs) replaced the Q and the Guy FCX, supplemented by a prewar ex-Burton on Trent single-deck Arab and three quite new Arab coaches. This was a period of extraordinary activity. At least two of the Gilford PF166s gained Perkins P6 engines, whilst one sported a Guy radiator for a time. Both the Daimler CF6s were fitted with P6 engines, with one getting a Guy radiator and later a Gardner 4LW. A Bristol B ran with a Gilford radiator, and the AJS Commodore was throughly renovated, in the process gaining a further P6.

Ernest Parish

Parish's fleet ran under the name "Felix Motors" and his colours were red and black, changing from the late thirties onward to maroon, red and cream. It is not known when the limited company was formed.

Water-borne transport was the principal interest of the Parish family. Ernest Parish began operating a bus locally in 1921, but details are sketchy. His first licence from Doncaster was for the Armthorpe service in September 1924 with a 20-seat Daimler, new in

>> *Opposite page lower: A replacement for the Guy six-wheeler came in November 1933 as YX 4527, a Guy FCX with a fascinating history. New to the Public Omnibus Company in December 1927, it became GS14 of the London General Omnibus Company two years later. The body was destroyed in a fire at the LGOC s West Green garage, but the chassis was salvaged and sent to Hall, Lewis for a new 60-seat outside-staircase body. It was then sold to the West Herts Motor Service of A B Slade. Blue Line bought it and some time later replaced the four-cylinder engine with a Lycoming unit from a Gilford. About 1943 it went to Barnaby of Hull, who reconditioned the body and enclosed the stairs. It is shown here in 1947, and it soldiered on until December 1948. (Author)*

Above: **UK 2399** was the first double-decker for any Doncaster independent. It was built and first used by Guy Motors as a Model BX demonstrator. It was shown when new at the 1926 Motor Show and was bought by Blue Line in July 1927. It worked on the Armthorpe route until 1933 when it suffered a serious engine failure. The Reynolds Brothers label presumably means that it was painted by them. *(Author s Collection)*

1921 as a lorry, although his headquarters were in East Lane, Stainforth. The Daimler was followed by a 14-seat Guy. In December 1925 he obtained a licence for Doncaster to Thorne Moorends (which Felix always called Thorne New Village) via Edenthorpe. During the next few years he had a Dodge, a Reo and three Thornycrofts, all 20-seaters. He moved to Dunsville in 1930, garaging the fleet behind his house. The buses carried a picture of Felix, the cartoon cat, on the sides.

The first full-sized bus, a Leyland Lion LT1, came in 1930, and was the first to carry a fleet number (9). It went to the War Department in 1940, returned and gained a new Barnaby body in 1943. There followed an AEC Regal, a Maudslay ML3E and a 20-seat Bedford. In 1933, an AEC Regal coach arrived which became another wartime Barnaby rebody, this time as a centre-entrance double-decker. A Leyland Lion LT7 came next, fitted with a Gardner 4LW engine from new, as detailed on the log book. A programme of converting the full-sized buses to either AEC or Gardner oil engines had been completed by 1938. Two more Barnaby-bodied vehicles were a Leyland Tiger TS7 dual-purpose and a Dodge SBF bus. The arrival of No. 15 in 1938 was a momentous event: it was a Roe-bodied AEC Regent, the first double-decker bought new by any local independent. This did 17 years of sterling service before being sold to Skills of Nottingham.

Almost all Felix buses were bought new, and kept in immaculate condition, although there was one exception, because of the pressing need for extra capacity in wartime. A very different AEC Regent came from South Wales, lowbridge WN 4751, which had a 5LW engine and the reputation of being one of the slowest performers ever.

In August 1941 Felix bought the "Renown" service of Mrs N Smith, thus gaining an extra share on the Moorends route. In early days Walter Smith, another Stainforth operator, had various services, but his staple route was the "Top Road" to Thorne, first licensed in 1923. He had died in 1937, with the business being carried on by his widow. At the takeover there were three buses: a singularly unprepossessing Dennis Lancet, an Albion Valkyrie and an Albion Victor, all of which passed to Felix, but

were sold off within a couple of years. Traffic increased as the aerodrome at Lindholme came into use, and an unfrozen Leyland TD7 and a Daimler CWA6 joined the fleet in wartime.

Felix appeared to have orders already in place, for 1946 saw the delivery of an early Leyland PD1/Roe and an NCB-bodied AEC Regent. In the following three years an AEC Regal III and three Leyland PS1s arrived, all bodied by Barnaby, together with a splendid Roberts-bodied AEC Regent III. All these postwar purchases were sold on and had long lives elsewhere.

THE THORNE VIA EDENTHORPE ROUTE

In addition to Severn, Felix (and Renown), one other operator, the last independent on this road, was Harold Wilson.

Harold Wilson

Wilson's vehicles fleetname was "Premier" and the colours dark blue and cream. The limited company was formed April 1934.

Harold Wilson's Premier was another Stainforth-based operator who did not serve that village. Unlike Felix, the premises remained in East Lane for the whole of the firm's long existence. Harold Wilson, who was married to Gina Parish, Ernest's cousin, is believed to have been the pioneer operator on the Doncaster - Edenthorpe - Thorne "Top Road" route. The fleet was never large until expansion took place in the 1950s. Services started in 1924, like so many others with a 14 seat Ford, with another and a Reo the next year. Then came two more Reos and a Thornycroft, all bodied by Clark of Scunthorpe. The big bus era began with a Leyland Lion LT2 in 1929, followed by a Lion LT1 and a Lion LT5, each with a different style of Roberts body. Barnaby rebodied the LT5 in 1943, and the LT1 was heavily rebuilt. Both survived till 1951. After a five-year gap a Bedford WTB appeared, followed in 1939 by an Albion Victor with Barnaby's attractive dual-purpose body. The double-deck requirement was met in 1940 by UG 6318, a 1933 Guy Arab from Leeds, followed by a wartime Guy Arab 2.

In the immediate postwar period the fleet remained quite small, though this was to

Above: The last prewar bus in Harold Wilson's Premier fleet was this smart little Barnaby-bodied Albion Victor, registered **DWU 216**, dating from July 1939, and seen here on 12th June 1948. After ten years' service, it was sold on to Ben Sketcher of Swinefleet.

Below: Loading up for Armthorpe on 30th April 1955 is **EWU 223**, Felix No. **22**, a wartime Roe-bodied Daimler CWA6, new in November 1943. The duplicate behind is **EWR 423**, the "unfrozen" Leyland TD7. *(Both: Author)*

change later. Three Guy Arab 3 double-deckers - NCB-, Barnaby- and Guy-bodied - replaced prewar saloons, with a Plaxton TSM coach coming from Fieldsend of Salford.

LAST OF THE LINE

E R Dodd

Using the fleet name "Selwyn Motors", Dodd's colours were grey and red.

Selwyn Motors is the last survivor of the erstwhile Christ Church operators. E R Dodd began his Saturday market-day express service from Belton in 1935 with a 20-seat Bedford WLB. That was replaced in 1943 with the 26-seat Dodge which had been with both Felix and Severn. Unfortunately this elegant little bus was destroyed by fire in 1948. During wartime and for a while afterwards, Dodd ran a daily service from Doncaster to Sandtoft aerodrome, and the Dodge was joined by a Bedford WTB and a Maudslay ML3.

Expansion followed in peace time. There was a Bedford OB bus, the ex-Felix Leyland Lion LT1, a Guy Arab from Burton, a Commer Q4 and an elderly, much-travelled AEC Regal 4 which was given a new Brookes body in 1949.

OPERATORS SOUTH OF DONCASTER

ROSSINGTON

G H Ennifer

Ennifer adopted the fleet name "Blue Ensign" and used blue and cream as the colour scheme for his vehicles. The limited company was formed in May 1932 (but see below).

George Ennifer was a wiry little man, unhappily burdened with two club feet, which did not appear to affect his driving ability or his enterpreneurial spirit. A large estate, known as New Rossington, had been set up to house miners working at the lately established Rossington colliery and their families.

Ennifer's story is complex, but began simply enough with a Saturday service from Doncaster in October 1920, using a convertible 14-seat Ford. During the 1920s, among others, he used three Vulcans, two Thornycrofts, a Karrier, a Dennis and a Leyland Lion PLSC in the Blue Ensign fleet.

In 1929 he began an association with Ernest Auld Heath, who at that time ran buses from Doncaster to Skellow based in Bentinck Street, Doncaster, and B. & E. Motor Services (Bentinck & Ensign) was set up. This concern, which later became B. & E. Motor Coach Services Ltd, began working a London to Bradford service, later working to Leeds after the purchase of Wilks Parlour Coaches. By this time Ennifer had left the company and its numerous vehicles were licensed to E A Heath. The firm, together with South Yorkshire Motors, became the basis of the London, Midland & Yorkshire Services Ltd in 1933, subsequently selling out to the Yorkshire Services Pool in November 1934. Heath also sold his Skellow service to Yorkshire Traction about the same time. In his own name Ennifer also possessed an express licence to Hanley, principally for miners and their families. How often this ran is not known.

Meanwhile Ennifer & Farmer Ltd had come into being, a short-lived partnership with Ed Farmer, who ran from Harworth into Doncaster and had some excursions and tours licences. A couple of AEC Regals had joined the fleet, but subsequently financial problems arose. In 1932 the company G H Ennifer Ltd was formed, the directors being George Ennifer and V P Packer. Vernon Packer was Ernest Heath's brother-in-law, and the capital came from Heath.

Trouble returned in 1939 when a receiving order was issued against Ennifer, who sold his house to repay his debts. He left the board of the company and was replaced by Mrs F A Packer. From then until his death in the 1950s, George Ennifer remained in the employ of the company which bore his name as a driver. One of the two 1931 AEC Regals went to the Air Ministry and was later stolen and never recovered. The second was rebodied and all three Regals later gained oil engines. The only wartime addition was a Bedford OWB.

Once the war was over there was considerable activity. Three very different double-deckers appeared: a 1932 ex-Leeds Leyland Titan TD2 which went into service with an AEC oil engine, ex-London Transport Q4, with a centre-entrance Weymann body, and a new Crossley DD42/5 bodied by Scottish

Above: **FDT 202**, Ennifer's Crossley DD42/5 with Scottish Commercial body, new in March 1948, is shown here decorated for the Queen's visit to Doncaster in 1952. *(Author)*

Below: **DT 2459** was one of two Barnaby-bodied Tilling-Stevens chassis delivered in June 1930 to Bentinck & Ensign for use on the Bradford to London service. It was last recorded with Farnsworth Motor Services, Blackburn in 1939. *(Author s Collection)*

Commercial. The coaching side was developed; a Duple Vista Bedford OB was followed by three Crossleys, a Maudslay Marathon 3 and an AEC Regal III. Between 1946 and 1950 the fleet more than doubled.

John H Barras

This operator ran as "Don" and the colours were red and cream. It is not known when the limited company was formed.

In May 1919 Ribble Motor Services was formed by Major H E Hickmott, John H Barras and a Mr Chapman by the purchase of James Hodson's business. Just over a year later there was a dispute. Barras resigned and returned to his native Yorkshire. In June 1921 he obtained a licence to run Doncaster to Rossington with, inevitably, a 14-seat Ford. Various early buses included a Vulcan, a 30-seat Leyland which ended up with Blackburn Corporation, an AEC 503, a Thornycroft A6 and Leyland Lions of both PLSC1 and PLSC3 specification. Buses were housed in a garage behind his house in Bawtry Road, something unthinkable nowadays in such a select neighbourhood.

A 1932 Leyland Tiger TS4 survived to be rebodied with its second Strachan body in 1950, and there was a Leyland-bodied Tiger TS7 and a Tiger TS8 coach. The workhorse for several years was the 39-seat Allsop-bodied Leyland Cheetah LZ4. Rossington timings seem to have been largely unaltered during the war years and single-deckers usually sufficed. Patrons had a useful choice for several years. Don's red Leylands, Blue Ensign's AECs, Rossie's green Daimlers and (often) the Corporation's Bristols. In 1944 Barras bought one of Severn's old Leyland lowbridge TD1s. At this stage all his vehicles were petrol-engined.

An interesting vehicle appeared in 1946 in the shape of a 1931 Crossley Condor which had been given a new "streamlined" style body by Manchester Corporation's Car Works in 1940, and to which Barras fitted a Perkins P6 engine. An even older ex-Manchester Crossley, a lowbridge, came next but didn't last long. The first new purchase was a Leyland-bodied PD1, though this was followed by a Crossley DD42/3 with Scottish Commercial body.

William Morpus

The fleet name was "Rossie" and the vehicles were painted green and cream. The limited company (Rossie Motors Ltd), came into being in March 1952.

William Morpus was a Derbyshire man who worked as a deputy at Rossington colliery. He had begun running by September 1923, like so many others with a 14 seat Ford. There were two Reos and, surprisingly, a Barnaby-bodied Bristol B. The love affair with Daimlers began in 1930 with the purchase of a new Daimler CF6. An ADC came from Wrexham & District, followed by three more CF6s from various sources. A lasting memory is that of the Rossie pulling out of Waterdale leaving its trail of blue smoke. In 1938 a Roe-bodied CP6 arrived from West Yorkshire Road Car. This was scrapped in 1944 after a serious accident on the A1, and replaced by a Daimler CP6 double-decker which had languished at the back of Doncaster Corporation's depot for some time, engineless. Its very dated Roe body was replaced later by an ex-Hull English Electric one. A further Hull purchase was in 1945 with another CP6 double-decker, this time with an English Electric body of its own. There was also a new Bedford OWB in 1943.

Morpus remained wedded to Daimlers, with two Plaxton bodied CVD6s and a Willowbrook one, together with a double-decker with a Barnard body replacing older stock, though the last CF6, which had already had two bodies, gained a new Brookes coach body and a Perkins P6 engine.

FINNINGLEY AND BLAXTON

T S Madeley

The fleet name "Premier" was used and the colours were blue and white.

In 1921 Thomas Madeley of Branton was running a 6-seat Ford van. A 14-seat bus was licensed by him for operating Doncaster Waterdale to Auckley in October 1922. The service was later extended to Finningley via Blaxton, and he subsequently owned a Ford T, a Berliet, a 14-seat Morris, Guy and Saurer 26 seaters and a Dennis G. Four vehicles were owned in January 1931. Madeley later moved

Above: **BDT 284**, the 37-seat Leyland Cheetah LZ4 of Don Motors, was the mainstay of their Rossington service for several years. Delivered in May 1939 with a body by Allsop of Sheffield, it remained with the company until late in 1957. This is a July 1951 picture. *(James Firth)*

Below: Although 17 years old, **GYG 205**, seen here on 2nd May 1965, still looks smart and survived for another three years. William Morpus liked Daimlers for his Rossie fleet, and this one had a Willowbrook body of a pattern found in many parts of the country. *(Author)*

his premises to Beech Grove, Blaxton. A number of excursion licences from Doncaster were obtained in 1934. That year saw the arrival of a new Roberts-bodied Leyland Lion LT5a which gave sterling service for 16 years. Another new purchase was a Bedford WTB coach. Second-hand came a Lion LT1 and MS 8837, one of the TS1s rebodied in some style by Alexander. At some point Blaxton cross roads became the terminus, the route running via Finningley aerodrome, very active in World War Two. This necessitated the purchase from London Transport in 1940 of RX 4351, a lowbridge Leyland Titan TD1 with outside stairs. A Bedford OWB was a further wartime addition. There was also a market day service to the village of Wroot. Madeley and Heath (Leon), the other operator on this route, had at one time been fiercely competitive, but notably closed ranks when Enterprise and Silver Dawn arrived in "their" territory.

In April 1946 a Manchester Corporation Car Works-bodied Crossley Condor appeared, quite a curiosity when it later gained a Perkins P6 engine and an Atkinson lorry radiator, then came an ex-Leeds Leyland Titan TD2 and a Birmingham utility Guy Arab 2. Two Strachan-bodied Crossley 42/5 coaches were bought new in 1949, but Tom Madeley decided to retire and the business passed to Leon Motors in December 1950.

F A Heath

The "Leon Motors" fleet name graced vehicles in a turquoise and cream colour scheme. The limited company was formed January 1947.

Leonard J Heath was first noted in 1923 based in Bessacarr with a 26-seater conveying workers into Doncaster from Finningley and Wroot. By 1924 the business was being conducted under his wife's name, Florence Amy Heath, and two 14-seat Fords and a Lancia were added. As a result of an illness contracted during his war service Heath was at times unstable. He had attempted suicide, been prosecuted for assaulting Tom Madeley and his brother Bruce, and had been the subject of complaints to the Traffic Commissioners. The business thrived, however, with two Chevrolets, a Laffly and a new Albion PM28 being added in the 1920s. It moved to Blaxton,

then Auckley, before settling in the grandly named Finningley House in the late 1930s. The routes were similar to those of Madeley, with in addition a Saturday service to Misson. A varied selection of second-hand vehicles appeared in the 1930s: a Dennis G, a Commer Corinthian, a Gilford 166OT, and at least three Leyland PLSC Lions. Another new Albion, a Victor PK115, came in 1935. Remarkable was a Leyland Lion LT5a coach which was rebodied as a centre-entrance double-decker by Northern Coachbuilders in 1943, while still retaining its 4-cylinder engine. Two early Leyland Tigers and a Lion LT5 followed with, early in the war, a Short-bodied highbridge Leyland Titan TD1 from London Transport. The final arrivals in wartime were two Bedford OWBs which saw a lot of use for a number of years.

T R Rees became manager in 1946 and remained so for many years. Various second-hand double-deckers came and went: a centre-entrance Leyland Titan TD2, a Leyland-engined Daimler CP6 from Bury and three assorted AEC Regents plus a Regal from Halifax. Excursions and private hires were developed with modern coaches: four Daimler CVD6s and two Bedford OBs came into stock, as did six of Madeley's vehicles.

OPERATORS NORTH OF DONCASTER

SOUTH KIRKBY & WAKEFIELD

United Service

This was an association of operators which was formed in November 1926. There were five equal shares: one for L L Cooper, one for W Everett, one for Newsholme Brothers, and two for J J Granter (one for himself and one shared between his son Jackie and his son-in-law Alfie Staff). Those concerned were all based in the mining villages of South Elmsall and South Kirkby. Established in 1918, Granter began running from South Kirkby into Doncaster in 1923 on a return-ticket-only basis, gaining a Doncaster licence for this service in 1925. The others ran in the opposite direction, from the two villages into Wakefield. After the association was formed it was subsequently possible, using Granter's licence, to initiate a through service from Doncaster to Wakefield.

Above: Tom Madeley bought this early Leyland Tiger for his Premier fleet in the late 1930s. **MS 8837** had been new to Alexander as fleet number P40, and was one of a batch rebodied by them in characteristic style. It is seen here in June 1948, subsequently passing with the Madeley fleet to Leon Motors. *(Author)*

Below: Another Madeley vehicle which went to Leon, and here pictured with them, was ex-Manchester Crossley Condor **VU 6293**. New in 1931, its Car Works body was reconstructed in 1939 after an accident. Madeley bought it in April 1946, and in 1949 had it fitted with a Perkins P6 engine and what appears to be an Atkinson lorry radiator. *(James Firth)*

Staff appears to have left the organisation around 1933, when his AJS Pilot (which later appeared with R Store) was sold to Cawthorne of Barugh. In 1931 there were eleven buses licensed by Doncaster, most of which were Granter's, though this probably included Jackie and Alfie Staff's vehicles. For a time before the war fleet numbers were carried, known ones of Granter were 9-12/4-16/9-21. Cooper had 17/8, but Everett's did not carry numbers. Vehicles generally carried the fleet name "United Service" and colours were a greenish blue and blue, although earlier Granter's had been blue and black.

Lawrence Lee Cooper (by 1931 Cooper Brothers, with Walter Lee Cooper)

The Coopers were grandsons of George Baum, a pioneer South Kirkby owner who ran his 1913 Karrier charabanc to Barnsley once a week. Lawrence Lee began in his own right in April 1923 with a small Ford, later taking Baum's Karrier. Then came a 14-seat Karrier, four Reos of assorted types and a Thornycroft. A 32-seat Gilford 168OT arrived in 1930. Two Maudslays, a 1931 ML3 and a 1936 39-seat Marathon, were the mainstays of the Cooper service through most of the 1930s and the war years. Their premises, originally in Stocking Street, later moved to Mill Lane.

A new Willowbrook-bodied Daimler CVD6 joined the Maudslays in 1947, with the older one being replaced in 1947 by a Burlingham-bodied AEC Regal III from Florence of Morecambe.

William Everett

Little is known of the early years of this operator. He was active on the South Elmsall to Wakefield route with a 14-seat Reo in 1926, in the next year buying a 20-seat Laffly. Two Gilford 166OTs came in 1929, both bought new, as were his remaining prewar purchases, a Dennis Lancet and two Dennis-bodied Lancet 2s, the second of which had a Gardner 5LW engine from new. Both survived until the early 1950s.

The year 1947 saw the arrival of a Barnaby-bodied Daimler CVD6, one of only three vehicles bought new among the many

purchased in postwar years. The old Dennis Lancet came from Granter, and there was an ex-Ribble Leyland Titan TD1 which had acquired a Gardner 5LW engine and was supplanted by a Daimler CWG5 from Barrow. A Daimler CVD6 with Plaxton bodywork and a fully fronted AEC Regal were added at about this time.

John Joseph Granter

Granter's first address was Saxon Mount, South Kirkby, but he had moved to Upton by 1931. His early activities have already been mentioned, but he is also known to have owned a mixed assortment of vehicles: four Reos, a Leyland, a Gilford 166OT and a 20-seat Mercedes-Benz. More variety came with an AJS Commodore and a 32-seat Crossley. In 1933 Newsholme Brothers sold out to Cooper and Granter equally. They owned two Maudslays, one of which was sold on, the other becoming part of Granter's stock. A smart fleet was built up in the 1930s, and this included a Dennis Lancet, four Dennis Lancet 2s and a Dennis Arrow Minor, a Bedford WTB, a Leyland Lion LT5a fitted with a Gardner 4LW from new and two Daimler COG5s with attractive Duple bodies. The only wartime addition was UG 5104, the unprepossessing and well-travelled Dennis Lancet which originated with Smith of Stainforth.

The first double-decker came in 1946 in the shape of an ex-Sheffield Leyland TD4, but fleet renewal began in earnest the following year with four Daimler CVD6s: two Willowbrook and two Duple coaches. In June 1949 the business passed to W R & P Bingley, who already had a coaching operation and one small stage service in the area.

ASKERN, MOSS & FENWICK

Thomas Walter Holling

This operator's colours were blue and cream.

In 1921, Verdon Holling of the Red Lion Hotel, Askern, began running between Doncaster and Askern with a 14-seat Ford "covered top wagonette", which lasted until 1928 when it was replaced by a Chevrolet. This operated on a Bentley council licence, and

Above: Cooper Brothers were the owners of the United Services Willowbrook-bodied Daimler CVD6 **GWR 168**, new in October 1947. Several of the group's buses were labelled "U S", which hardly seems a good idea.

Below: Everetts purchased a total of 49 buses in postwar years, of which only three were bought new. The first of these was this Barnaby-bodied Daimler CVD6, **FWR 968**, in February 1947. It was sold to Beehive, Adwick le Street, in 1956. *(Both: Author)*

probably ran only on market days. At that time there were other operators on the Askern road, notably Bennett, who sold out to Bullock & Sons, with services through to Pontefract, Selby and York. By the mid 1920s the owner was Thomas W Holling of Moss Road, Askern. The route was extended to the villages of Moss and Fenwick, and the Traffic Commissioners granted a licence for this service, Saturdays only, which continued for the next 36 years. A Bedford WLG was owned, and later a 26-seat Bedford WTB. The final acquisition in this period was a Bedford OWB in 1944, though there was a considerable expansion of Holling's activities in the postwar period, which began with a couple of Duple Vista Bedford OBs and a Leyland PS1 from the Barton fleet.

APPENDIX

Those independent concerns which sold out before 1939 to municipal or large company operators do not appear in this account. Some were quite significant, like J Guest of Swinton with his Doncaster - Rotherham and other routes, which was jointly purchased by the two Corporations and Barnsley & District in 1928, and F Bennett of Askern, whose Doncaster - York and Doncaster - Pontefract services went to Bullock & Sons in 1929.

Barnsley & District, later Yorkshire Traction, mopped up the others to the west of Doncaster in 1929: Francis Stewardson and G S T Deverew, who ran to Goldthorpe and Thurnscoe. To the north they took Ernest Auld Heath's Skellow via Woodlands route (a separate entity fom B. & E. Services mentioned earlier) in January 1935, and Thomas Septimus Camplejohn's similar service which ran via Bentley.

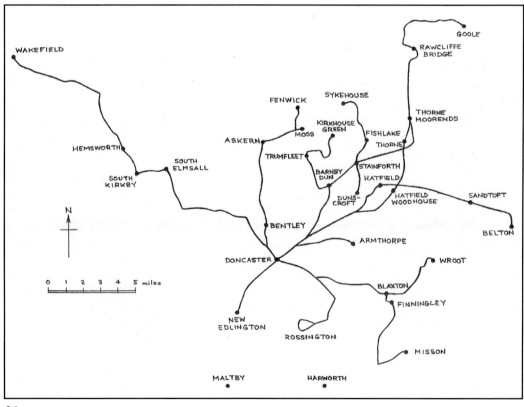

Above: GWW 49/50 were the last purchases by Granter before his portion of the United Service was sold to W R & P Bingley in January 1949. They were Duple-bodied Daimler CVD6s, and **GWW 50** is seen in Wakefield in 1954. *(Author)*

Below: In prewar days Thomas Holling's market day service needed only a small fleet, the newest of which was this Bedford WTB, **DT 9468**. *(Geoff Clarke)*

Above: With just four months left to go, Store's 21-year-old Dennis Lancet **YG 642** looks very run down. It has had a larger destination box and new opening windows fitted, but the Guy radiator it acquired in 1950 neither fits nor improves its appearance. *(Author)*

Below: **BWY 978**, Store's 1937 Leyland Cheetah LZ2, has one of the few bodies built by Barras of Stainforth. It remained in service until 1954. *(Geoff Clarke)*

28

Above: Store's neat little Barnaby-bodied Dennis Falcon, **GAT 226**, came in August 1939, just before the outbreak of war. It gained a Perkins P6 engine in 1948 and was sold on in 1950. *(Geoff Clarke)*

Below: **JWX 261** was the second of the Barnaby-bodied Leyland CPO1 Comets ordered by Store primarily for the Goole route. It was delivered after the Morgan takeover in August 1950, but in the Reliance livery, and was the last bus to survive in these colours. *(Author)*

Above: Pictures of the Q types are hard to come by. This is Store's **AML 996**, the ex demonstrator bought from Leeds in 1940. The photograph was taken in April 1949 when the vehicle had become very dilapidated. This was its last month in service before becoming a static caravan at Dunscroft.

Below: May 1949 saw the arrival of the replacement for the Q. This was **HWX 3**, a Guy Arab III with Meadows engine and Barnaby body. Note the outward similarity to the contemporary Roe product. This bus later gained a Gardner 5LW engine. *(Both: Author)*

Above: One of the Leylands (either an A9 or a Z5) with which Severn built up services in the mid nineteen-twenties. It was not uncommon at the time for vehicles to be fitted with pneumatic tyres on the front and solid at the rear. The use of boys as conductors was also common in those days. *(Author s Collection)*

Below: **CM 8737** was one of a pair of Leyland TD1s bought by Severn in late 1939. New to Birkenhead Corporation in 1930, they had passed through the hands of Wilts & Dorset. A third joined them in 1940 and, despite the lowbridge layout, they were the backbone of the wartime service until the arrival of the utility Guys. *(Author)*

The second of Severn's Leyland PD1s, **FWW 480**, seen when brand new in 1947. It had a Northern Coachbuilders body and was rebodied by Roe in 1955, ending its days in Scotland with Steel, of Stevenston, a member of the A1 collective. *(Both: John Banks Collection)*

Above: Severn's **BWW 692** was a Leyland LT7, new in 1937. It was rebodied by Barnaby in 1949 as shown, and gained a Leyland 7.4-litre oil engine. It was later sold to a Welsh operator. *(Author's Collection)*

Below: In the four years 1946-9, Severn bought nine brand new Leylands. **JWR 531** was one of a pair of Yeates-bodied Tiger PS1 coaches which came at the end of 1949. Both passed to Meller of Goxhill in 1958. *(Author)*

Above: The "Blue Canoe" was **WU 5893**, a Reo Pullman new to R F H Wilson's Blue Line in April 1927. It was sold in 1933.

Below: This little Bedford WLB, **WX 9494**, seen in an unknown location, was new to Blue Line in January 1932, and was sold to Tyler of Wallingford in 1937. *(Both: Author's Collection)*

Above: The final fling of the Gilford company was the PF166, with its early type of Perkins engine and 32-seat Park Royal body, and a low unladen weight of 4 tons 7 cwts. The concept was similar to that of the Bristol SC many years later and with more resources behind it could have been a winner. **AWT 514**, new in April 1935, was the first of three owned by Blue Line, all of which gave long service, particularly on the Goole route, to which they were ideally suited. This photograph was taken on Marine Drive, Scarborough. *(G F H Atkins)*

Below: A more common type of Gilford was the 168OT. **GP 5147** of this type was new to Main Lines in London in 1931. After a spell with Kemp Brothers, Withernsea, it passed to Blue Line later in the decade. It is shown here as rebodied in wartime by Barnaby and it survived in service until 1950. One of Severn's Leyland LT7s is seen behind the Gilford. *(Author)*

Above: Another Blue Line wartime rebody by Barnaby, of a curiously high build, was on **CTO 188**, a TSM Express that had been new as a Watson-bodied coach to Bees (Nottingham) Ltd in March 1937. Photographed in April 1952, it moved on for use by a fairground showman in 1954. *(Author)*

Below: Shore Brothers, a Doncaster garage and coach operator, had two similar Daimler CF6s, **DT 1655** (seen in another Scarborough view) of 1930 and DT 2315 of 1931. Both were given more up-to-date coach bodies by Plaxton in the late 1930s, as shown on the next page. *(G F H Atkins)*

In 1941 Shore Brothers withdrew from the coaching market and sold DT 1655 and DT 2315 to Blue Line, who initially used them in their green livery. The top picture was taken in 1947, just before **DT 2315** went for a rebuild which included the fitting of a Perkins P6 engine and a Guy radiator. The lower shot shows the detail alterations to the body and the new radiator, but by this time (June 1950) the Perkins engine had been replaced by a Gardner 4LW. It ran for another two years in this form. *(Both: Author)*

Above: An odd Blue Line purchase was this 1930 AJS Commodore from Chapman's Ivy Coaches, of Huddersfield, which arrived in Armthorpe in 1942. Converted to wartime perimeter seating (30 + 30 standing), it reverted to normal layout early in 1948, when the body was renovated in Blue Line's workshops and it acquired a Perkins P6, yet never managed to gain a Guy radiator. *(Author)*

Below: **EWW 683**, new in March 1945, was the third of Blue Line's wartime Guy Arabs, this time with a Northern Counties body. It led an uneventful life and was withdrawn in 1958. *(James Firth)*

Above: January 1949 saw the arrival of Blue Line's first postwar double deckers, HWU 437/8, which were Guy Arab IIIs with Meadows engines and Guy bodies. They both gained Gardner 5LW power units about 1955. **HWU 437** is shown. *(Author)*

Below: Blue Line bought several second-hand post-war Arab single-deckers. **JTF 763**, a Barnard-bodied example, was almost new when it came from J Guy, of Ketley Bank, in October 1948. *(James Firth)*

Above: Pictured in Thorne, **WW 3239** is one of several Thornycrofts bought by Felix in the 1920s. An A2 model, it was new in August 1927, later passing to a Blackburn operator. *(Author s Collection)*

Below: **AWT 170** was Felix No. **14**, a Leyland LT7, which, according to the log book, had a Gardner 4LW engine from new. Delivered in April 1935, it had a Barnaby bus body, and on withdrawal in 1950 was sold for works transport to British Ropes, where it survived for another seven years. The picture was taken in September 1949 on St Leger Day, when services from the east side were not allowed into the town, but had to terminate about a mile away in Norborough Road. *(Author)*

Felix No. **9** (**WX 3297**) is shown as delivered in March 1930. A Leyland LT1, quite early in its life it received a Gardner 4LW engine. From 1940 to 1943 it was with the War Department. On its return it went to Barnaby for a new body, as pictured below in 1948. It was sold to E R Dodd in July 1949. Behind it is **WN 4751**, the Gardner-engined AEC Regent bought from South Wales Transport in 1941. *(Author s Collection; Author)*

Above: Felix **BWW 560**, a 1937 Leyland TS7 Tiger, had a well-proportioned Barnaby dual-purpose body. Originally petrol-engined, it had a Leyland oil engine fitted in 1950, and in total gave Felix 20 years of service. When this picture was taken it was already 17 years old. As delivered it was numbered 13 but, perhaps for superstitious reasons, later became No. **18**.

Below: Postwar Barnaby dual-purpose bodywork had more curvaceous lines. Felix No. **27** (**HWX 899**), an AEC Regal III 6821A, was delivered in September 1949. It was photographed in Armthorpe in 1953, and in 1956 was sold to Harold Wilson. *(Both: Author)*

Above: An unfrozen Leyland Titan TD7, Park Royal-bodied **EWR 423**, came in 1942 as Felix No. **21**, serving until 1956. By this time the cat emblem had disappeared from the buses. *(James Firth)*

Below: Felix's first postwar purchase was **EYG 33**, an early Leyland Titan PD1 with Roe body, in July 1946. In 1958 it went to the Ayrshire A1 group, members of which bought several ex-Felix buses. *(Author)*

Above: June 1950 saw the arrival of Felix Motors Ltd's Leyland-bodied PD2 No. **31** (**JWX 259**), which was sold on to Derwent Coaches of Swalwell in 1966. *(Author)*

Below: An interesting view inside the Horbury works of Charles Roberts shows prominently Harold Wilson's **YG 1030**, a Leyland Lion LT5, with its bodywork under construction. It was delivered in June 1932. *(Author s Collection)*

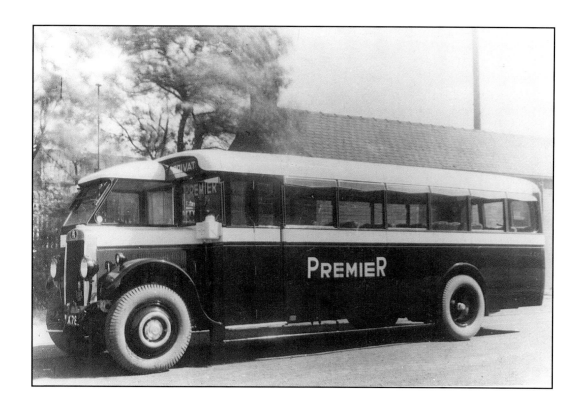

A Charles Roberts of Horbury body of a different pattern was fitted to **WX 7897**, Harold Wilson's 1931 Leyland Lion LT1. It was completely rebuilt and reseated in the late 1940s, passing to a contractor in 1951. *(Author's Collection; The Wakefield Collection)*

Above: **UG 6318** was a 1933 Gardner 6LW-engined Guy Arab with English Electric body, which came to Harold Wilson from Leeds City Transport in August 1940. Hardly handsome, from 1944 to 1948 it sported a Leyland radiator which did not improve its appearance. It was withdrawn in 1950. *(Geoff Clarke)*

Below: New to Harold Wilson in May 1947, Guy Arab III **FYG 44** had a Gardner 5LW engine and a Northern Coachbuilders body. *(Author)*

Above: **JWR 184** was another Wilson Guy Arab III, this time Gardner 6LW-powered and bodied by Barnaby. It came in November 1949.

Below: Purchased by Wilson from Fieldsends of Salford in October 1949, when it was just over a year old, **DBA 634** was a smart Plaxton-bodied TSM K6LA7. It ended its days at the Borstal Institution in Hatfield. *(Both: Author)*

Above: E R Dodd bought **FRT 581**, a 1946 Commer Q4 with body by Myers & Bowman, in February 1950, selling it three years later to an operator in Burton on Trent. *(James Firth)*

Below: Four of these prewar Brush-bodied Guy Arabs came from Burton on Trent into the Doncaster area, and Dodd had two. **FA 6419**, new in 1936, was taken into stock in January 1949. *(Author)*

Above: Bedford OB **MWB 310** was the longest serving member of Dodd's fleet. Bought from E H Sims of Sheffield in May 1953, when it was withdrawn in 1971 its long-serving driver decided to retire with it.

Below: New to Ennifer in March 1937, **DT 8378** was an AEC Regal with an unusual style of Burlingham body. Originally petrol-engined, it later gained an AEC oil engine. The picture was taken in September 1949, some 18 months before it was sold to Scarlet Band of West Cornforth. *(Both: Author)*

Above: **BPG 507** had been bonnet number Q4 in the London Transport Country Area fleet. It had a Weymann centre-entrance 53-seat body, and arrived with Ennifer in July 1947. By the time this photograph was taken in 1951 it had been fitted with an oil engine and the front had been rebuilt by Hartley, a local coachbuilder.

Below: Ennifer had three Crossley coaches, two bought new and this Strachan-bodied 42/7 model, **GGE 452**, which came from Cotters of Glasgow in 1949. *(Both: Author)*

Above: John Hubert Barras of Don Motors liked his Leylands. This Tiger TS4, **WX9727** is pictured when new in December 1931 at Strachan's works. *(Author's Collection)*

Below: The same vehicle, when 18 years old, went back to Strachans for a new coach body (and a Covrad radiator), retaining its petrol engine. It was withdrawn in 1959, aged 28, after an accident. *(Author)*

Above: The Leyland metal-framed body on Don's **DT 7466**, a Tiger TS7 new in June 1936, does not seem to have been as troublesome as some of that type, lasting in service until 1959, although it was on hire to the E.W.S. during the war, returning in 1945. *(James Firth)*

Below: This Crossley Condor, **VU 3645**, was new in 1931 to Manchester Corporation, who gave it this new Car Works rebody in 1940. Don purchased it in April 1946, and retained its " streamline" livery. It gained a Perkins P6 engine in 1947, and on withdrawal in 1950 ended its life as a static caravan. It was photographed on 4th September 1948. *(Author)*

Above: Don's first new double-decker, an all-Leyland Titan PD1, came in October 1947. **EDT 680** passed with the business to East Midland in April 1962, but was not used by them. *(John Banks Collection)*

Below: Don bought **ASN 62** from Brown of Garelochhead in November 1950. A Crossley DD42/3 with a Scottish Commercial body, it had been new in December 1946. *(James Firth)*

Above: Seen when new in March 1926, **WU 4871** was a 26 seat Reo Pullman with Barnaby body, and was the second Reo in the Rossie fleet of William Morpus, with whom it served until 1934.

Below: Seen at Charles H Roe's factory is Daimler CH6 demonstrator **WX 8098** when new in 1931. West Yorkshire ran the vehicle from new, although it was recorded by them as "property of the Daimler Company". It passed to Morpus (Rossie) in 1938, and gave useful service until being written off after a serious accident in August 1944. *(Both: Author s Collection)*

Above: Rossie **FV 1003** is seen at Doncaster Racecourse with its third body. A Daimler CF6, it had been new to Bracewell of Blackpool and had a 26-seat Burlingham body. Rossie bought it in 1934, and it was rebodied as a coach by Fielding & Bottomley. It gained a Perkins P6 engine in 1947, and two years later was rebodied by Brookes of Dinnington, being withdrawn in 1956. *(James Firth)*

Below: Rossie's **RH 6118** was a 1934 Daimler CP6 with an English Electric body. The vehicle came from Hull Corporation in August 1945. On withdrawal in 1951 the body was transferred to a brand new Daimler CVD6 chassis as KWT 600. *(Geoff Clarke)*

Above: This Daimler CVD6 with Barnard body, **HWX 753**, was Rossie's first double-decker bought new. It was photographed in Doncaster on 29th August 1964, its humble duties contrasting with those of the Alexander-bodied Leyland Leopard coach alongside, which had called in for a refreshment stop on an express run from Scotland to the Capital. *(Author)*

Below: Tom Madeley's brother Bruce stands proudly beside the Barnaby-bodied Guy **WU 9718**. New in 1927, it served Premier for 10 years. *(Author s Collection)*

These Charles Roberts official photographs show Madeley's **AWA 674**, a Leyland Lion LT5a in brand new condition in July 1934. The roof-mounted luggage rack was later removed. After withdrawal the vehicle went to a showman in 1950. *(Author s Collection; The Wakefield Collection)*

Above: Madeley's last new vehicle was **HWX 775**, the second of a pair of Strachan-bodied Crossley SD42/5 coaches that had been new in May 1949. It passed to Leon as their No. 26 in December 1950, not longer after this September 1949 photograph. *(James Firth)*

Below: Taken in June 1948, this rather indifferent photo shows Leon No. **7** (**JP 42**), possibly the only Leyland Lion LT5a double-decker. It began life in 1934 with Smith's of Wigan as a Santus-bodied coach. Leon bought it in the late 1930s, and had it rebodied in utility style by Northern Coachbuilders in 1943. It survived in this form until 1950, when it became a caravan. Note the emergency repair to the upper-deck front window. *(Author)*

Above: In July 1927 Leon took delivery of this Albion PM28, **WW 2577**, seen here at Roe's Crossgate works. The vehicle was sold for use as staff transport to the Crown Bedding Company, Birmingham in 1937.

Below: Leon's second new Albion, some eight years later, was this Victor PK115, **AWU 461**, with coachwork by Barnsley Motor Bodies. When a fleet numbering system was introduced, it became No. 1. It was withdrawn in 1949. *(Both: Author s Collection)*

Above: Leon No. **5** was **EWT 952**, one of two Duple-bodied Bedford OWBs, new in 1943. Taken on 7th March 1953, this picture shows that it had been fitted with upholstered seats, though the "streamlined" painting style hardly disguises its utilitarian shape. *(Author)*

Below: **GK 5715** was London Transport bonnet number TR26 before passing to Lansdowne Coaches of Fleetwood. A 1930 Leyland Tiger TS1, it gained this elegant Plaxton coach body in 1938 before passing to Leon in March 1939 as No. **4**. It was photographed in July 1951. *(James Firth)*

Above: Leon bought several Daimler CVD6 coaches, including No. **12** (**JNN 420**), a 1948 example with Plaxton body. Behind is one of the ex-Madeley Crossleys in this photograph dating from 25th May 1958.

Below: For a period Leon bought ex-Halifax AECs to a total of one single- and three double-deckers. No. **14** (**JX 5263**) was the first, a 1937 Park Royal-bodied example with an 8.8-litre AEC engine, which came in September 1948. It was photographed in Doncaster, waiting to leave for Finningley, on 28th June 1952. *(Both: Author)*

Above: The coachbuilder of **WX 8430**, Cooper Brothers' Maudslay ML3, is unknown. New in September 1931, it remained in regular use until its withdrawal in 1950, and was still smart and well-kept when seen in Wakefield in June 1949.

Below: Now splendidly preserved, **JTB 749**, a Burlingham-bodied AEC Regal III, is usually associated with Florence Motors of Morecambe. Indeed it was with Florence, but it spent just two years with them before passing to Cooper Brothers in June 1950 and spending 17 years in their fleet before going for preservation. *(Both: Author)*

Above: Seen here in Doncaster's gloomy Marshgate bus station, **GWT 540** was one of a pair of Willowbrook-bodied Daimler CVD6 buses new to Granter in October 1947 and withdrawn in 1961, by which time this route was served by double-deckers.

Below: Thomas Holling's first "big bus" was **HVO 125**, a Duple-bodied Leyland Tiger PS1, which came from Barton Transport in May 1949, when just two years old. It was given a full front in 1952. *(Both: Author)*

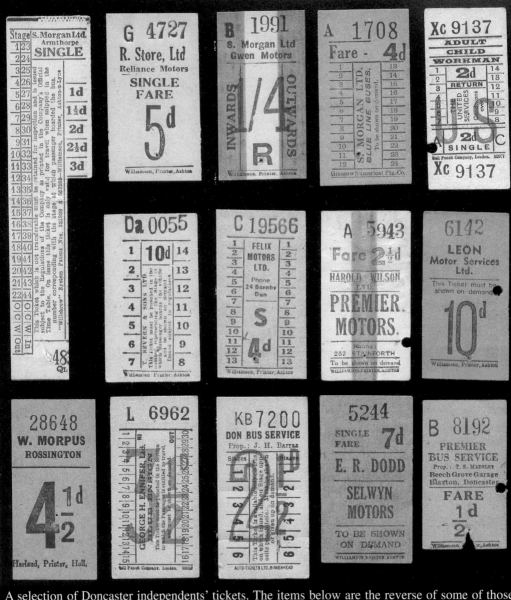

A selection of Doncaster independents' tickets. The items below are the reverse of some of those shown above. Five different printers were responsible for this small range of tickets.

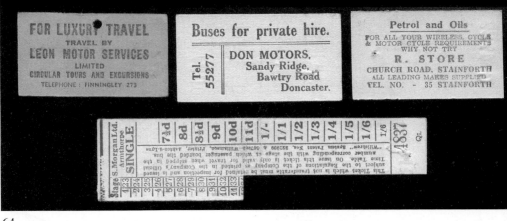